SpiritPoint:

Balancing the Six Aspects of Life

Daniel J. Red Goldstein

with Laneshia A. Lamb

Table of Contents

Note to Readers

We are born, we live, and then - we die. Simply put, hearing, seeing and feeling such a timeline can seem grim. But what if you create an extraordinary life for yourself? What if you live with purpose instead of letting chance direct your life? What if you choose intention, exist in gratitude, and pour yourself into your passions. And, what if you take care of your body in a legit there-are-no-second-chances kind of way? How much differently would you read it: *we are born, we LIVE, and then we die?*

If you're anything like me, I bet your entire mood would lift if you knew you had the power to direct life as you desire versus letting circumstances dictate their terms to you. When you discover how your purpose in life stands inside a magical space where opportunity and optimism meet, your atmosphere will transform from ordinary to charged. Taking control and directing your purpose in life is exactly what the SpiritPoint System provides.

As I discovered the system you are about to embrace, I learned how mastering the process of being reflective and proactive could bring a sense of constant renewal to anyone. Tapping into my strengths and feeding them into where I felt most vulnerable gave me more power to live on my terms than I'd ever imagined. As you join me on this journey, you will learn how to transform your life by organizing, connecting and balancing what I call the Six Aspects of Life: Spiritual, Mental, Physical, World, Family and Career.

As you work your way through these pages, you will discover how to take inventory of your life using the SpiritPoint System. Every occurrence in your life, day in and day out, has some kind of impact whether positive, negative or neutral.

Inventorying is the process in which you quantify and qualify differing aspects of your life, with the intention of understanding how to effectively organize and integrate them all. When you take a few moments each day to become stronger in all facets of your life, a greater sense of fulfillment will be yours. Like everything in life, you rarely reach perfection, you enhance the journey.

Utilizing this book begins with understanding the theory behind the SpiritPoint System. The program functions by showing you how to bring balance to all aspects of your life. The more harmony you bring to the details within your personal space, the more you take control of defining and executing your purpose in life. The hexagonal graph, with all its interconnected lines, features the Six Aspects of Life on its corners and shows how everything in life is connected. The convergence in the middle of the diagram represents the point where your spirit achieves balance and you feel the success life has to offer.

The first step on this journey is to complete the pre-assessment with regard to YOUR Six Aspects of Life. The workbook format you'll see laid out, creates your own personal space to write in the pages. Get messy! Get creative! Let loose! There is no need to share your information with anyone unless you choose to do so.

Taking the pre-assessment provides you a gauge of where you stand with regard to the program before digging into the rest of your reinvention journey. The scale is small, using numbers one through three. This will give you a quick visual of where to start. As you'll see further in the book, each aspect has six areas within, featuring the same self-scoring system. You'll see thirty-six areas of your life, full of your own details, all in one document.

The most amazing part will be when you begin to see how each area within each aspect connects with everything else. The hexagonal graphs in each section serve as your gathering point. Blank lines to the side of each hexagon provide space for you to organize, connect and renew as you begin to make use of your own information.

You'll also see references throughout the book to the *happy account*. As you identify positives you discover or create within each aspect or area, you'll add those powerful tools to your *happy account*. When life deals you a challenge in ANY aspect or area, you'll be able to draw upon your *happy account* to help solve the issue, whatever it may be. *Happy account* is a fun name for a very serious notion and is at the heart of what makes the SpiritPoint System function.

As you'll see when you complete your pre-assessment, most of us start off with a less-than-balanced life. If you draw a line between each scored aspect or area, you will most likely see a picture that looks like a wobbly wheel. That's OK. Just know, as you work the program, you'll begin to smooth out those wobbly wheels and move forward more efficiently.

So, congratulate yourself! You're like the rest of the world...with one major exception. You are now taking the steps needed to bring more balance into your life. You are taking control of defining your purpose.

Six Aspects of Life – Pre-Assessment

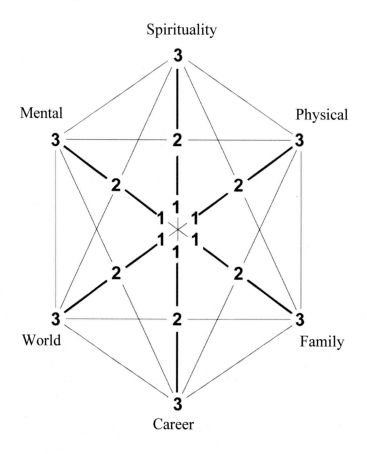

1 - Negative
2 - Neutral
3 - Positive

Introduction

The sun was shining brightly; it was one of those days when the weather was perfect to do just about anything. It was 1989, I was a couple years into my new career, and in that moment, things felt right. I was at the YMCA, swimming laps in the pool when I realized I was at a really great place in life.

Had someone asked me two years before if I saw myself there, they would have found my answer in the midst of my laughter. After 25 years, I had left the family business, a place where I had sown and quite frankly, I was waiting to reap. I guess the world had a different plan for me, because the business I thought would be mine was now in my rearview.

As I sat poolside that day, I realized things were going well. I would even go so far as to say I was experiencing euphoria. I felt light; my mind was clear, and I am pretty sure I could leap tall buildings. I felt that good.

I remember sitting there reveling in my own satisfaction, only to be brought down from my high when I returned home. My recollection of exactly what jarred me from my euphoric trance is blurred. Perhaps I stumbled over one of my son's toys, or received an unexpected bill. Whatever it was, there was an obvious shift in my atmosphere from a state of seeming perfection back to normalcy.

Over the next couple of days, I attempted to retrace my steps. I wanted to understand what that feeling was; I needed to get back there or at least understand what there was. What I found in my moments of reflection was that I had been suspended in wonder as a result of a powerful balance I had unconsciously reached. So, I took to my notebook, attempting to empty myself of everything I knew to be true at the time.

I was blown away. When I looked down at the pages in front of me, I realized there were patterns. I am a doodler; it's how I mentally cleanse. And, the poolside experience sent me into overdrive. I began to organize my thoughts, and noticed there were words and concepts that kept repeating themselves across the page. Hours later, I realized everything fit into one of six distinctive groups. The most amazing part was, beginning to see how every segment of my life was connected in one way or another.

My euphoric experience led to an epiphany; I realized my life was made up of all the little things within it having purpose. And the more I assigned purpose to everyday matters previously seeming unimportant, the more fulfilled I became. Actually, all of us can discover these connections when we put our minds at ease and allow the patterns to be seen. In our own way, we are always working towards one goal or another in these same groups. Now the question is:

do we do so with the intention of achieving our purpose in life?

Imagine for a second, you and I are in the same room, and instead of reading these words, we are having a conversation. I want you to open your mind; I am going to ask you a question, and I urge you to avoid thinking too deeply as the answer is right under your nose. In front of you are two seemingly different items, a diamond and a couch, both valued at $5,000. Which of the two is more valuable? Take a second, just a second, and think about it. Before reading on, write down your answer, or at the very least, have it in mind.

Since I had the pool encounter back in 1989, I started sharing the patterns I saw and the potential for self-renewal with others. I wanted people in my circles to experience what I felt or to at least have the tools for mapping out for themselves how to get there. And in my sharing of what I had discovered for myself, I have always asked the 'diamond and couch' question. Over the years I've received many different responses with well thought out reasoning as to why.

Here's the deal. They both have the same **dollar** value. Sure, many may argue the perception of the diamond as being more valuable. After all, it's a girl's best friend. Others may argue that the couch has many uses or is bigger, making it worthier. But the fact of the matter is, they both are valued at $5,000, and despite any elaborate explanation, they're equal.

Determining financial equality is easy when it comes to items having nominal value, but what about the experiences, people and even items in our lives we most often refer to as priceless? That's where subjectivity comes into play, because obviously, the matters we care about may be valued differently if we ask someone who had little physical or emotional ties to them.

So, why the couch and the diamond? I am sure the thought crossed your mind. I wanted to pick two seemingly opposite items, to really get your mental wheels turning. I wanted you to be able to see the truth for what it is, while also experiencing that split second when you over-thought it all. Existing inside that split second is your subjectivity. In that crevice of thought is where your own feelings and experiences start to impact how you view the things in front of you.

But, what if you got into a habit of training your thoughts and feelings to process your life more purposefully? The lamps in your home have purpose because they shine light where there is darkness. The pen in the bottom of your purse has purpose because at some point, you will need it to write down important thoughts or ideas. Even the frames in your home or office have purpose because they display the photographs of your friends and family, whom you love so dearly. Everything has a purpose, whether tiny or rarely used. Our responsibility to see and understand this concept becomes front and center in our lives.

Imagine feeling a deep sense of accomplishment in whatever you do, whether grand and complex or mundane and simple. Imagine dealing with any negativity affecting your life in such a way you could always count on your own creativity to find peace of mind - in every circumstance. Finally, imagine tying all of this together in a process resulting in a sense of life-long fulfillment and joy, and maybe even an occasional bout of poolside euphoria. You achieve the results you want by balancing the Six Aspects of Life.

Balancing the Six Aspects of Life

Happiness is not a matter of intensity but of balance, order, rhythm and harmony.

- Thomas Merton, Social Activist

The Six Aspects of Life, as I've laid them out, are not meant to place any more emphasis on any one area than another. Instead, my goal is that, by the end, you will be mindful of their interconnectivity. When I decided to move forward with writing this book, I did so with some hesitation. For years, I had been having conversations and facilitating trainings on the material. Quite frankly, I had grown used to the comfort of being face to face.

Because creating a book forces a distance, I kept second guessing how to start it, what to put in the middle, and how to end it. Then one day I realized, "I will write the book as if I am face to face with its reader." With that in mind, this is our conversation. Most importantly, it is your journey; map it out as you see fit. I want you to start where you feel most led. I also want to create an experience allowing you to immediately feel impacted or driven to *do* any action in a mindful way.

Recall the couch and diamond exercise. The diamond is the concentration of power into the smallest space with the most impact. For example, let's say there is a family member you really enjoyed growing up. You always had loads of laughs and enjoyed each other's company, but somehow, over the years, you two had grown distant. One day you decide to call him or her out of the blue. How much value do you think your conversation will have?

I tried the above scenario with an associate of mine, and what resulted was more frequent family gatherings. A telephone conversation lasting fifteen minutes has now impacted her, her uncle, and the rest of the family who also attend Sunday dinner. The happiness stemming from my challenge to her to give her uncle a call, expanded into other aspects of her life.

The couch in this scenario is the ordinary usage of time and effort of everyday life. We need ordinary time like we need a place to sit. But, we generally don't see unremarkable occurrences as special. For some people, everyday life is simply not mindful. The call to my associate's uncle lasted only fifteen minutes and her day at work took eight hours. When we discussed her call afterwards, we both agreed the conversation with her uncle and her day at work had equal value, but the time differential was huge! The mindful call to her uncle took some extra thought, and the results are still reaping joy. One kind and conscious act continues to spread joy and renewal throughout her family. It's the *doing* that starts a domino effect of mindfulness.

Studies have shown, if you practice conscious thought just 20 minutes a day, over a four-week period, your brain chemistry will evolve allowing a more sustainable path to happiness. Careful consideration of all your actions is the main tool for building your *happy account* . The more good you do, the better you feel, and the more *goodness* you'll have available for utilization when future circumstances call for such a need.

If we can agree there's a 100% chance something bad will happen at some point, imagine the difference in your reaction when you have a large available balance in your *happy account* versus having none.

Here's the reality: negative occurrences in our lives take a toll on us. In some instances, they force us into hiding. For others of us, we maintain our normal lives but do so with masks on. Ask yourself, are either of these situations healthy? One is taking for granted that help could be a phone call away - a listening ear from a friend or family member, and if need be, a counselor. The other is a disaster waiting to happen, as we bury deep the situations, feelings, and emotions we choose to avoid. We end up wearing a mask of pretend, making it seem like we're okay, when the truth is, we aren't.

Fulfillment is why the *happy account* is crucial. We all need a place from which to pull peace. When bad happens, your *happy account* will act as a buffer against the dark. As we go about creating, making use of, and constantly adding to our *happy accounts*, we need to see how they work using the SpiritPoint System. Therefore, let's a take a quick look at the Six Aspects of Life. Each will be discussed in further detail as you go through the book.

Spirituality has a different meaning for everyone. For some of us, spirituality is outward, by way of organized religion. For others, it's inward, a personal and, oftentimes, private experience. Even some agnostics and atheists can attest to an order existing greater than themselves.

Once you realize the impact of spirituality on the other aspects, you also realize the power you have that can be immediately exercised. Teal Swan, founder of the Headway Foundation, defines spiritual practice as a shift in perspective. An action as simple as closing your eyes and taking a deep breath can center you and provide clarity in unclear situations. For believers, it's divine Providence instantly answering your call. For others, it's nature or the cosmos lining up with your receptors allowing power to enter.

Family is all about connection and presence. When was the last time you connected with a loved one who you haven't seen or spoken with in a while? Better yet, how often are you connecting with family, even those in the same household? Before you say you connect every day, let me offer a deeper perspective of connecting. If you Google the word connect, you will find several definitions, but the overall idea states someone is joining or meeting. For the sake of this conversation, it's with the intention of building or deepening a relationship. Connecting with your family is more about them than you. It's about allowing them to talk, learning more about them and discovering the happenings in their lives. The connection you initiate is about creating a space of comfort. The end result is valuable for all of you.

So, again I pose the question, when's the last time you connected with a loved one? If you really connect, there's a

100% chance it will bring you happiness, even if just for a moment. And, each time you continue to connect, reflect upon how it makes you feel and the impact it has on your family member. The power of the connection becomes exponential, and the value becomes priceless.

Mental is centered on intentionality. I currently have a plan in place where I hold myself accountable for learning a new fact, idea or way to improve every day. The new lesson I teach myself can be minor, but must be relevant to one of my varied interests. I remember a children's song called "Knowledge is Power" by Teresa Jennings. Her lyrics included, "Knowledge is power. I know what I know. The more you learn, the further you'll go." Wow! Some kids' songs ring true, even for adults! When we exercise our brains, we feel more confident as we navigate through various opportunities. I challenge you to do the same.

Physical is the reflection of the saying, "*your body is your temple.*" Cliché, right? Even so, it's true. Trainers will tell you, the moment you feel like giving up is the precise moment you have to push yourself harder. Whether you're an exercise enthusiast, a foodie, or the person who has been planning to make an adjustment physically, you understand the importance of taking care of your body. Certainly, there's a link between your physical wellbeing and the other aspects of your life.

Everything about us... affects everything about us. The sooner you take steps to make the interconnectivity of all the aspects of your life more positive and purposeful, the more power you will have.

World is a reminder: love conquers all. Do you believe this to be true? For some of you, your mind went immediately to romantic love, and maybe you thought to yourself, *"There were a few things love didn't conquer."* I hear you, but consider this: if love is in the action, and if we set out each day to act in love, how conquered would our problems be? Showing love includes those we know and perfect strangers, the people we pass on the street. Imagine, if instead of ignoring that person you walked past in the hallway this morning, you smiled and said "hello." What impact would you have had? Let's take it a step further: the person you passed in the hall was having a bad day and your smile helped to brighten his gloom. Now, how much impact did you have? The fact is, the impact of our actions may remain a mystery, but at least we can rest assured, we've done our part.

Career is the foundation upon which all the other aspects rest. We all can agree, money is necessary. Even more necessary than money is responsibility. Imagine if you spent ten less dollars each week. How much would you have saved at the end of the week? Only ten dollars, right? Now, multiply ten by fifty-two and you have easily put away an extra $520 at the end of the year…without really doing much differently! However, the responsibility tracks you lay down by saving even this relatively small amount of money are quite valuable. Imagine putting a savings discipline to work for several future needs and wishes.

Take it a step further and cut out spending on items you know you don't need. Where would you be in thirty days, six months, or a year? What will your savings afford you, what new opportunities now lie ahead of you?

Many of us know how much income to expect from one month to the next. Use that information to plan for not only your current need, but also your future needs. Rocket science is not needed to understand the importance of a healthy financial foundation for yourself. Support for the other five aspects of life will rest on that foundation when you secure it with proper funding and spending. Being mindful of your financial foundation is another testament to how one aspect of life affects and feeds into all the others.

The SpiritPoint System lays everything in life out on a six-point hexagon, balanced on its bottom point rather than laying on one of its six sides. At the top of the Six Aspects of Life hexagon is *Spirit*. At the bottom is *Career*. On the left side are *Mental* and *World*, top and bottom. On the right side are *Physical* and *Family*, top and bottom.

Spirituality is at the top because attaining an understanding of the Holy One or the universe is priority for most people. *Career* is at the bottom since all other aspects depend on a foundation of sound money practices. The left side features the concepts interacting with our public facing (*Mental*, *World*), and the right side is composed of the more private decisions we make (*Physical*, *Family*). The top half (*Mental*, *Spiritual*, *Physical*) is all about the individual. The bottom half (*World, Career, Family*) is all about the individual's relations with others.

The more we can balance all the intricacies and activities of the Six Aspects of Life, the better life will be. As we dive deeper into each aspect, be thinking of how you can be adding to the *happy account* within each. Knowing how to balance it all will begin to reveal new opportunities for greater satisfaction as you work through the program.

Spiritual

"Spirituality is meant to take us beyond our tribal identity into a domain of awareness that is more universal."

- Deepak Chopra, Humanitarian

Since the dawn of time, there has been the belief that a power greater than us exists. The thought in itself provides comfort for many of us knowing, a power greater than us is out there providing the Grace we sometimes feel we don't deserve. Spirituality is a big part of people's lives, whether or not they engage in typical or traditional religious practices. We have become a society that has taken our own interpretations and made them work for us and our lives. Of all the Six Aspects, *Spirituality* is the most enduring and deserves its place at the top of the hexagon.

For many years, I questioned the existence of anything. You could say I was skating on the cusp of atheism. So much was happening in my life I just didn't expect. At the tender age of fifteen, I was rebellious. I had let my hair grow out. I surrounded myself with a few friends who were not the bring-home-to-mom-and-pop type. I had even begun to drink alcohol and steal. I was a good child, gone wild.

At the time, my parents were separated. I lived with my Dad in Texas while Mom was in Philadelphia. I didn't understand what was going on with them. I just knew I didn't like it. Without Mom home, things were different. Dad was physically present, but he was emotionally adrift. I ended up mostly fending for myself. Now, as an adult, I can see how the lack of proper supervision took a toll on me physically and mentally.

Along with my unwanted, but newfound independence, and buddies in situations like my own, I took on a grungy look, and some rather unsavory practices.

In those days, there weren't many constructive activities kids my age could do without proper guidance. And, as you can probably guess, that rarely ended well. I am certain the lack of appropriate recreational choices contributed to our mischief.

Most of my newfound friends and I lived near an abandoned golf course. We found ourselves there one hot summer Friday night. We were drunk out of our minds as we celebrated a triumphant week of thievery. That particular week it was lawnmowers and bicycles. We wanted to create minibikes, pretty much the only thing we could rely on for transportation. Although they were illegal, we were never stopped, and we were on them frequently as we went to our various hangouts.

It was an intolerably humid Friday night. My life changed forever as the sky was clear; the stars seemed to multiply across its darkness. We partied and drank until our bodies laid across the green, a colorful mixture of drunkenness and sleep. Startled, I woke from my slumber. I looked at my watch and realized nearly four hours had passed. My eyes were wide open, not the typical late-night activity you would expect from a drunk teenager who was passed out moments before.

There I was, wide-eyed, staring at my friends as they continued to snore. I felt clear and focused, a feeling I had yet to experience. The effects of the beer had long gone.

As I stood, marveling at the brightness of the stars and contemplating the vastness, I allowed my mind to drift and experience traveling to the furthest star, wondering what lay beyond. For the first time, it dawned on me, perhaps there wasn't a 'farthest' star. Perhaps the sky continued on endlessly into infinity.

Imagine the degree to which my mind was blown. All at once, my vision became clearer. I could see more and I could also conceive more. I know what you're thinking, I was *tripping* as a result of being drunk, but no that wasn't the case. I was completely sober, taking in the wonders of the world. My mind went into overdrive as I processed the whole concept. I looked around me, and there were my friends, still asleep. And, suddenly I felt so distant. I was soaring among the stars, and they were on the green, among our discarded beer bottles.

Time went on as I found myself lost in my discovery. If infinity existed, could the same be true for the entity people called 'God'? The questions flooded my mind, and in that same instance I felt a tug at the top of my head, as if it were opening like a formerly clinched fist, ready to receive. I compare the experience to a massive download. I stood there suspended in time as years of information seemed to fill me and drive me numb. Although there were no angels playing trumpets, my vision was incredibly clear as if the presence was now confirmed.

I have told many people of my experience. Some of them believed the phenomenon was nothing more than the side effects of my drunken state. Others attributed the experience to my subconscious desire to confirm the mysterious. And, then there were those who chalked it up to an active imagination of an otherwise rebellious fifteen-year-old.

As for me, I believe it was divine intervention. The experience caused me to question how I was living my life.

Yes, even as a teenager, I felt compelled to clean up my act; the time had finally arrived for me to quit the gang. I remember being so lost in my powerfully bizarre episode that I didn't realize one of my friends had awakened. His voice came in closer from the distance, *"Hey Goldstein, what's up with you?"* I simply smiled and said I had to go. I can still see his puzzled expression, but it didn't matter. I knew what I had to do.

It was still pretty late, or pretty early, depending on your perspective, when I arrived at my parents' house. For the first time in a long time, it felt like home. I walked inside and into my room, but I couldn't sleep. My eyes were wide open, and so was my mind as my heart raced.

Over the next few hours, I went through what seemed to be an involuntary internal rehabilitation. I began to take notice of details of life like I'd never done before. I made a pledge to God and myself, my life's course would be different. The time to put away childish and rebellious antics had come. Instead of chasing after evil, I was ready to embrace the promotion of joy.

Oftentimes, I wonder if my golf course experience was the initial domino for the chain reaction that followed. In a matter of days, Mom called and told Dad she was coming home. She was ready to make amends. A few days later, she was in her old red Rambler wagon, pulling into our driveway. Seeing her was different this time around. I was filled with love for her, and I showed her in an embrace like none other.

Funny thing is, had this been pre-golf course, I would have spoken out against her, scolding her for leaving me. But on that day, her previous whereabouts didn't matter. She was my mom and I her son, and I was just excited she was home.

That next school year, I entered tenth grade with the promise I'd made lingering in my every thought. I was determined. I ended up on the honor roll and was elected to be my high school's representative on the city-wide student council. I continued on my upward track. By senior year I had become president of the council and an integral part of decision-making for the school district. I was keeping my word, and it felt good.

School wasn't the only place where I wanted to exercise my redirection. I wondered "what else should I do?" Was my experience a sign I should become a rabbi? Granted, I had a torrid past. I am pretty sure I was one of the worst students in my synagogue's Sunday school and bar mitzvah program. So, naturally I had no idea where to begin. Ultimately, I wanted to share my experience with others. I went to see the rabbi at the Reform synagogue I had attended all of my life. Perhaps you can guess the response I received.

I will be the first to admit I had made some mistakes growing up, many of which were known throughout my community, including within the synagogue. When I began to ask questions about becoming a rabbi, he thought it was a joke and blew me off. My rabbi seemed to disregard my experience on the golf course, and I was disappointed. I was changing, and I wanted a chance to show him how. I tried the Conservative synagogue in town. At least the rabbi listened a bit longer, but the results were the same. I was sent away, confused by the responses I received. And, I was even more confused with what I should do with myself.

Before I found myself in the great rebellion, I was in the Boy Scouts. During sixth grade, I was in the troop housed at the Disciples of Christ Church in my neighborhood. Quite frankly, it was my haven. The minister walked in one day and said, *"All of you boys are welcome as guests in our church, no matter what your beliefs are. We respect that you believe in God and that you are a Boy Scout. No matter how you see God. If it works for you, then it is good."*

This moment is memorable because it was the 1960s, a time of evangelism and anti-Semitism in Fort Worth. I was Jewish, and I was also very skeptical of Christian preachers. But this man was different. And his message echoed in my ears three years later when I wondered where I would go next and what I would do with myself.

I was nervous about going to see him. Anytime I had encountered Christian ministers previously, they tried to convert me. But, I was willing to take the risk, considering how open he was to others' beliefs a few short years ago.

When I shared my experience from the night on the golf course with Reverend Walker, the reaction I felt was different. This time around was sure to be unusual, and my thoughts proved to be true. Reverend Walker literally jumped for joy at my interest in being a rabbi. He told me, if I was serious, he would help me. The conversion speech never came. Instead, he told me he would help me find an appropriate seminary for my needs and guide me on my journey. He shared his belief that it was his duty to show me the ways of the Father as I saw Him, not the good pastor's way. He made me feel comfortable. I felt I could trust him.

Finally, there was someone who was willing to listen to me, and it appeared Reverend Walker understood.

My experience with this wise and kind minister influenced my development of the Four Phases of Religion, a crucial component to the spiritual aspect of life.

Four Phases of Religion

Religion is one of those touchy subjects many people choose to avoid. This social fact became more and more clear to me as I got older. Along with that clarity came the Four Phases of Religion, a theory I fell upon after I had my experience on the green. And over the years it has continued to grow and develop.

I believe four different kinds of people inhabit the earth. Although I am speaking specifically about religion, my concept can be applied to just about anything in life. The people who populate the Four Phases range a great deal depending on their openness to other folks' points of view. In some cases, they can be stubborn as a mule, or able to view the world through a selfless lens, and all points in between.

Do you remember the Danny DeVito children's fantasy comedy from the mid-1990s, "Matilda?" There was a scene when DeVito's character says to Matilda, *"I'm smart, you're dumb; I'm big, you're little; I'm right and you're wrong."* That line pretty much sums up Phase One. The people who exist on this plane believe they are right and you are wrong. They don't want to hear what you have to say. They are content with what they already know. And there is nothing you can do to alter their thinking.

The individuals in this phase are close-minded. They aren't interested in your opinions because, for them, you're wrong. Before you even have a chance to share it, they have concluded it has no substance. Having a conversation with such a person is pretty much out of the question when the two of you have conflicting points of view.

Phase One thinkers are constantly in a space of personal consideration only. Imagine how those around them feel, how disregarded their feelings must be. The same is true when discussing religion.

If you feel your opinion is the only one that matters, you stunt your growth by limiting the possibilities within the new information someone presents. You literally put a lid on how far you can go when you consider only yourself.

Phase One people act the way they do, oftentimes, because they have been beat up in life. Their behavior reflects how they protect themselves so they don't have to get out of their comfort zone and admit there's another possible way. They're just jammed up since they don't know how to get out of their own tight box they've built. Rather than be angry with them, keep looking for other ways to communicate with them. Patience is often the answer here! But, when persistent calm doesn't work, sometimes you just have to walk away from Phase One folks and hope they'll find their own way out.

Have you ever encountered someone who was verbally agreeable, yet internally skeptical? The person who gets quiet in uncomfortable situations or who changes the subject to avoid dealing with what's before them? They are Phase Two. Similar to Phase One, they believe their religion is right, and yours is wrong. However, instead of arguing or sharing how they feel about your religion, they alter the conversation.

They would rather talk about completely different subjects than to engage in a conversation for which they see no future. Their feelings are strong, but they just aren't the best at expressing them. The best way out is to get out.

Phase One folks can debate you under the table; they believe *that* strongly in their opinion. And, no matter what

52

you say, they will have a rebuttal for it. That's the major difference between them and Phase Two.

Phase Two people choose not to debate, and their refusal could be the result of any number of things: lack of confidence, fear of confrontation, resentment of authority, or simply avoiding responsibility for their thoughts and feelings.

Religion often involves relationships with others. When we close ourselves from the thoughts and opinions of family and friends, we forego any opportunity to serve others or have them be of service to us along our journey. If they are considerate, Phase Two people will often find ways to be of service that don't involve controversial subjects.

Phase Three

Phase Three thinkers believe what works for them gives them solace and what works for you brings you comfort. They are understanding. They get the meaning of consolation and its impact on a person's wellbeing. For them, the two of you don't have to agree and you don't have to be on the same page. You simply have to respect each other's differences.

This phase, obviously a step up from the first two phases, often lacks action. It's a feel-good phase because it creates a space of acceptance. People who exist here allow those around them to be just as they are. The question then becomes, now what?

Phase Four

Phase Three with a cherry on top is a good way to look at Phase Four. Not only do Phase Four thinkers respect the differences in people's beliefs, they also meet people where they are. Reverend Walker was a Christian, and I was Jewish, yet he never spoke of converting, even though many of his co-religionists would say he sinned by not doing so. He respected, not only the fifteen-year old kid in front of him, but the 3,700-year-old tradition I represented. Instead of trying to sway me, he provided solutions catered to my needs.

Phase Four is crucial to humanity; it involves recognition and understanding. It is also serving from a selfless perspective.

I often wonder where we would be as a society if more people existed in Phase Four. It expands far beyond religion. Recall the conversation I had with one of my associates, where she was directed to contact an uncle with whom she hadn't spoken in a while. The task was to call him and allow him the space to talk. There had been a family rift at one point, and the uncle had been set to the side, so to speak. Reaching out to her uncle was indicative of her own Phase Four existence. She put her own needs on the backburner to serve another person where he was.

As mentioned earlier, her results were amazing. They were able to reconnect, family dinners resumed, and her uncle was now in attendance. It's the simple things that go a long way.

Consider for a moment if we approached all our relationships in this manner. Instead of only thinking of ourselves, we thought of the needs of others as well. Imagine all the arguments that might end.

We stand the chance to deepen our understanding of the people in our lives just by listening. As simple as it sounds, too many of us neglect to do this on a regular basis. Life takes over, we become busy, less mindful, and as a result we unconsciously become selfish.

When we feel as though we are pouring ourselves into our careers, our families, even our relationships, sometimes we are tested. We think we fail because of being so caught up on reclaiming *our time*. Wanting good outcomes for ourselves does not make us bad people. Wanting good outcomes at the EXPENSE of others is more problematic, and certainly not within the spirit of the Fourth Phase.

There are the things we know because we can see them; we can touch them. And then there are the things we've been taught to believe in, far beyond what can be explained. For many of us, our belief exists inside of a construct, from which we can pull and to which we can refer. Even then, there is no proof to its existence. Yet we believe in it, we die for it, and live by it. These things I refer to as mystery, and it is the first component of spirituality.

In the summer of 2017, a friend of mine and I went on a very vigorous three-day hike in Colorado. It was one of those experiences where the anticipation builds as the leave date approaches. You get there and wonder why on earth you ever agreed to such a thing! And, after the adventure is over, you're glad you went.

In the midst of our vacation, I decided to venture off on my own. While my friend enjoyed top notch spa treatment, I walked through the woods. I remember reaching a point that prompted me to stop. And, I as looked out over the earth, it happened again. My poolside experience reintroduced itself when I least expected it. I felt happy, fulfilled, and most grateful for every aspect of the life I enjoy.

As I stood there, I recited a traditional prayer from my faith community. Reaching to God, it dawned on me. Religion is the tool we use to attempt an understanding of mystery. Worship is our medium we employ to connect us with a higher power. And, even if we never confirm its existence, we still feel good believing there exists a power greater than us. Trusting in a deity allows many people to live and lead a fulfilling life.

Over the years, it has become clear to me. This is how we reach Phase Four of Religion. By accepting that religion is how we communicate and connect with a higher power, even if our connections are different, one way is not better than the other. The heavenly connections are simply ours.

In fact, celebrating the other and recognizing their differences contributes to the beautiful, inspiring and mysterious complexity of our spiritual world.

Works

When we were born, we knew nothing of the world. We were innocent and completely oblivious to the ways of those around us. The things we know today, we know because we were taught, whether formally in a school setting or, informally, at home. And, even if you grew up sheltered, when you left home, you saw, experienced, or maybe even took part in an injustice.

There is no shortage of wrong in this world. The imperfections seem to grow minute by minute. And, guess who influences those misdeeds? We do. Our actions and inactions speak volumes about what matters to us. What causes do we support? What injustices do we notice? Do we turn away…or confront the wrong?

I believe we should repair the world a little bit each day. See a piece of trash on the ground? Pick it up! See a person struggle with a door? Open it for them! Hear a person utter a painful remark? Ask why they would knowingly say mean words. Then, listen to what they say. The ugly remark may simply be a cover for some injustice they experienced, possibly having nothing to do with their hateful words in the first place. To paraphrase a thought from *Ethics of Our Fathers,* 'although I didn't cause the brokenness, nor did you, we must do our part to repair whatever we see wrong'. Even if we never see the fruits of our labor, we must still do the work.

So, the question becomes, how do we repair the world? If we focus on all that is wrong with our planet, becoming overwhelmed is inevitable. The world needs so much attention. To be effective at making the world a better place, wouldn't your time be better spent if you could concentrate on just the few wrongs within your power to fix rather than the vastness of all the ills?

Having lofty goals is admirable, but the reality for many of us; we don't have the resources to *go big* right now. So, use what you have. In my readings and moments of reflection, I've identified a few things we all could do to *repair the world.*

One, give others their time. This means transferring that spotlight over your head to them. I've realized that I am uplifted by lifting others. Sounds cheesy, I'm sure, but it really works. Allow others the space to shine, support them, and give them a boost when they need a lift.

Two, ask someone how they are and actually listen to their response. I've seen, and even been, that person who's checking a box throughout the day. You know the person you pass in the hallway or in a parking lot, who asks how you are and keeps walking. Slow down and take the time to listen for the answer.

Three, be kind. Hold the door open for someone, help someone move a heavy object, and smile. You never know what someone is going through; your smile could be the game changer.

Four, take care of yourself. When riding a plane, the flight attendant always instructs passengers to save themselves first. The fact is, you can't be of service to anyone unless you're in good shape. Otherwise, you run the risk of losing two people instead of saving two. The same is true in real life; you have to take care of yourself before you can repair anything or anybody.

Five, be positive. There are enough negative people in the world without you adding to the list. Rather than dwelling on all of the things having gone wrong with your day, share what went well. By doing so, you will inspire others to be more conscious of their *good times* as well.

Six, don't judge. Just as the Fourth Phase of Religion states, accept people as they are and meet them where they are. What benefit is there in passing judgment on a person, or a decision, you won't have to live with, personally? People make choices based on what's happening in their lives. Be positive, smile, act with kindness, and allow them the space to be who they are.

Seven, learn new things. Not only does this strengthen you mentally, it helps you spiritually as you work to make the world a better place. As you expose yourself to new ideas, you become more tolerant and less 'judgey'. See how that works!

Eight, share your story. Whatever your journey has been, share the tale. There may be someone who is waiting to relate to you, someone who is waiting to not feel alone. Making the world a better place is accepting that it's not perfect. It's also accepting that we aren't perfect. Showing our flaws so others feel more comfortable with theirs can be a magic elixir. Imagine what we could do if we all performed just one action, every single day, that propelled us forward.

The experience I had as a teenager, on the green, laid the foundation for alone time. Even as I lay there, surrounded by drunken teenagers, I had an experience allowing me to silence the noise.

Life, as we all know, is filled with ups and downs. And, the best way to deal is to keep the good of the world front of mind. I'll be the first to admit, it's no easy task, but I once read, *between stimulus and response there is a space. In that space is our power to choose our response. In our response lies our growth and our freedom.*

This quote by Viktor Frankl, Holocaust survivor and author, really hit home for me. Unfortunate occurrences will happen in life. In between those occurrences and our responses to them, we have a choice to make, to see the bad or the good. We make the decision to be a victim or to be the victor; the opportunity to see life as 'the world' happening TO you or FOR you.

There are many choices, and most often they fall into one of two categories: positive or negative.

So, how do you train your mind to see the good, the positive? Take time for yourself. Meditate, and silence the noise around you. Look inward, and allow yourself to be elevated to new levels of mindfulness. When you arrive at a state of calm, you can look at any situation and find a way to make it better. Trying to find the good during a state of panic or even just ordinary time is difficult at best. A calm center you create through meditation is the launchpad for finding the good in any situation, and ultimately, harnessing that good for a new direction.

Meditation took some time for me to master. Being alone is easy, but quieting your mind is a task. Our lives are busy, and it seems there is always one more responsibility to handle or somewhere to be.

When we allow time to devour us, we suffer. In reality, time never speeds up or slows down. How we stage the use of our twenty-four-hour day determines our serenity or tumult. No matter the circumstances around you, the opportunity to set the schedule is always in your hands. Does this take practice? Are you able to implement such a plan immediately? Yes! When you decide your time is more valuable than the circumstances pushing you around, you will determine how to push back and make life happen the way you want it to go. Prioritization is the key. And, the best time to find your newfound ability to reprioritize? During meditation.

Examine your day as a set of slots needing to be filled with important endeavors…beginning with a time for meditation. Skeptics might call meditation the 'nothing at all' time. Nothing could be further from the truth.

Some will tell you the clock is always racing. Again, a lie. You are in charge of what fills the clock. You are in charge of what fills its minutes.

This is why meditation is so useful; it's a few deliberate moments in time where you allow yourself to slow down. You decompress. You relax. You believe. You experience. You get to know you. You smile a little more, you're a little more selfless, a little more generous. In this situation, you embody all that is well with the world. Especially, when you feel more in control of how to spend time for your most important initiatives discovered during meditation.

Prayer

If I don't first connect with God, I find difficulty in concentrating on self-improvement. Prayer is the act of connecting, and we all have our own way of doing so based on the constructs of our religions.

Although it is listed last, it is by far the most important component of spirituality. Prayer creates the space to connect with the mystery, it encourages the work, and it lays the foundation for meditation.

And, even if there is no scientific evidence for the existence of a higher power, researchers say prayer improves self-control. It improves your overall mood, and it makes you more accountable for your actions. The flip side of the coin, it makes you more forgiving of others. Prayer also makes you stronger and less susceptible to stress.

Consider, for a moment, the impact on your spiritual life if you became more intentional in all of your life pursuits. Tap into your belief system. Do the work that makes the world a better place. Take time to connect with yourself, so the good is prominent. And make the time to connect with whom you serve. How much will your life improve, simply by being more mindful?

As you assess yourself in the area of spirituality, it is important for you to ask yourself a series of questions. How connected am I? How intentional am I? How consistent am I? How persistent am I? Your answers will reveal your spiritual inventory allowing you also opportunities to fill your *happy account*.

I share my stories with you in an effort to highlight how common imperfection is. And it's okay. Imperfection is opportunity to improve. It is your catalyst in becoming your grandest self.

Spiritual

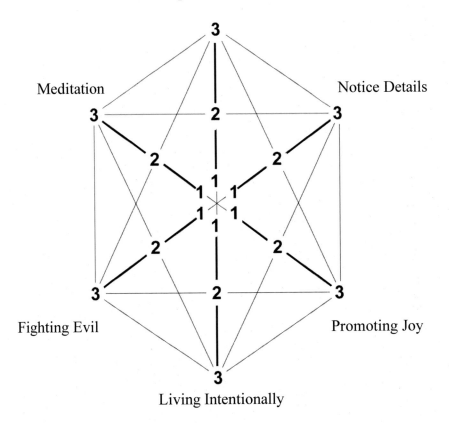

1 - Negative
2 - Neutral
3 - Positive

Mental

The strongest people are not those who show strength in front of us but those who win battles we know nothing about.

- Author Unknown

When the *mental* area of the Six Aspects of Life revealed itself to me, four areas stood out as equals: clarity, learning, creativity, and entertainment. Intertwined within each are confidence, and keeping mind-altering substances under control.

Our minds can be a source of strength or a constant reminder of where we fall short. *The strongest people are not those who show strength in front of us but those who win battles we know nothing about.* Reading this anonymous quote immediately solidified the importance of mental health for me. As I read it, I thought of the battles existing in our minds. I thought of the battles I encountered personally.

Those are the battles that catch people off guard. It is in the confines of our minds that we house the belief, we are strong enough to leap tall buildings or too weak to ever conceive the possibility of leaping. As Tom Rath shared in his book, "Wellbeing," the *single biggest threat to our own wellbeing tends to be ourselves.* We hold infinite power, if only we believe.

While in college, I had a bout with depression. There was a point in my life where I might have been embarrassed to admit that, but now I understand it happened for a reason. Outside of the fact I was young and trying to figure out life, I was overwhelmed. In the process, my physical health and mental health suffered.

I had been adulting for quite some time. Although my parents participated in my life to some degree, it just seemed they mostly had other things to do…which left me to do a lot for myself. I even had to finance my own education. So, I decided I would start earning my degree at the local junior college. My high school administration team, with whom I had become extremely close over the preceding four years, objected to my decision. This was my only choice. See, I was a good student, but merit-based scholarships only went to kids with better grades. And, since my parents had money that could have paid for college, qualifying for aid was out of the question.

I was in a bizarre corner of privilege keeping me from obtaining assistance while my own funds I had set aside would only buy a few semesters at best. Yet, I was determined to fulfill all my heart's desires. I started night school and had a job as a teacher's aide. I managed to save up enough money to pay tuition at the University of Texas at Austin. I was excited. My high school successes showed me I could accomplish just about anything and I carried that mentality with me to college.

With money in the bank and a good grade average from the junior college, I transferred to the university and my sophomore year looked promising. I was pursuing pre-law, I had a cool girlfriend, and my money issues seemed a distant concern. Or, so I thought. The year was 1973 and that fall was the Yom Kippur War when the Middle East erupted in violence causing oil prices to spike in the United States.

With oil shut off to our country, we were suddenly in the midst of recession and inflation. The money I had set aside for college was becoming pennies on the dollar compared to what I needed.

Life changed, and it appeared to happen all at once. By the time I began my junior year, my previous planning was crumbling around me. I was also 'enjoying' a bit too much beer and marijuana. My use of mind-altering substances was an escape from the confusing pain I was experiencing versus a healthy way to 'let loose'. By that spring, I found myself in a downward spiral of depression. My girlfriend seemed to demand more; my classes became more strenuous, and my grades were less than what the law school I wanted to attend would accept. With school expenses now growing out of my budget, I had to make some serious adult decisions.

I remember, like it was yesterday, walking through campus in a daze. I am certain I wore a look of defeat across my face as I contemplated my end. So much defeat, an angel stopped me and redirected my footsteps. I considered him an angel, although his day job was college professor on the university's campus. He must have seen in my eyes what I felt everywhere else in my body. He asked me if I was okay, I responded with a distant stare, unable give a reasonable verbal response. I thought I had had everything together. Reality had a different view.

He walked me to the Student Health Center and told them I needed help, staying by my side until a counselor would see me. The counselor helped me to stabilize myself to a point where self-harm was off the table as an option. Within a few days, I dropped out of school. The angel/professor had saved my life. However, my university education had come to an end. I am forever grateful for the angel/professor who stopped me, and pray someday, I'll either see him again to offer a powerful 'thank you' or simply be empowered to do for someone else what he did for me.

I moved home, and it felt like I had been sucker punched. One blow to the abdomen, and I keeled over, attempting to catch my breath. What had happened and how did it get this bad? I was the guy who could do it all. I graduated a student leader, worked my butt off to save up enough money to pay for college, and here I was back at home.

I thought I could handle anything and everything. And, even though I was beginning to feel the overwhelm, I figured if I just added more to my schedule, somehow life would become all better. Soon, I discovered my limits while also realizing I had little adult guidance to get me back on track.

Mom was an artist, and Dad was a jeweler. They both had their own lives which they struggled to intertwine with each other. It had been that way since I was fifteen. When life directed me back to my childhood room, the blow was devastating. I buried myself between my sheets. I had grown weary of adulting. I needed a break.

Days passed and the furthest I seemed to make it was to the bathroom, returning to my bed to burrow myself deeper in its comfort. Looking back, I realize my pillows were actually my shield from the world, prolonging the inevitable.

The truth was, I had to get up. Sure, the situation was difficult, but sleeping all day offered limited options for changing my circumstances. I had gone from being a troubled kid in middle school to the guy who'd completely turned his life around, becoming a student leader in high school. I had built relationships with administration officials some adults envied. I had even obtained responsibilities well beyond my years. To find myself there, between those sheets, became intolerable. My spirit began to revolt.

I finally found it within myself to get up. It was like a lightbulb went off symbolizing it was time. I continued counseling and began spending time at my dad and uncle's jewelry store. The plan was, I would work there for one year, learn a bit more about the family business, and then return to school the next fall.

If only I had a dollar for every time I had a plan that took a turn. After the first year, I decided to stay just one more year before returning to school. While I was there, I went from cleaning counters and sweeping floors to using my own jeweler's loupe, inspecting the gems, and cultivating a designer's eye. Those two years became twelve. I married, had a son, and needless to say, a university education remained 'in the future.'

My experiences have taught me, invincibility is for Superman and Batman. If I need help, I have to ask for it. Above all, it taught me the preciousness of good mental health.

In those years, as I worked hard to put myself through college, I saw my plans get rearranged out of my control. I learned it's easy to be led, and much more challenging to do the leading when it comes to our minds. It takes intention; it also takes courage and the insurance and assurance a full *happy account* provides.

My actions became more intentional. My pattern of speech adjusted as I carefully removed negatively infused words from my vocabulary. I redirected the way I thought, as I realized the impact limited beliefs could have on my future. I wanted to do all I could to preserve my mental health, now one of the four components of *mental.*

Even as I've now put pen to paper, I've had to take steps back to correct my language. I am intentional in my use of words evoking progressive movement and positive thinking over those translating to negativity.

I urge you to try infusing positive words into your own speech. Imagine if every time you had a conversation, you used only words that meant something good; then imagine the impact of those conversation on you and those around you. I've realized, caring for our mental health involves a shift in the way we view things. And the shift is intentional.

The famous American botanist, Liberty Hyde Bailey, once said, *"A garden requires patient labor and attention. Plants do not grow merely to satisfy ambitions or to fulfill good intentions. They thrive because someone expended effort on them."* This, albeit gardening based, is a perfect reference to how we should care for our mental health.

Our mental capacities require tending, meaning we must apply a considerable amount of effort to ensure its strength. Our minds gain strength when we exercise them in a way that yields those results.

Several years ago, I wrote an article for a service club magazine about what I called the *Five Ideals of Success*. Among the five was mental security. I shared that, being able to call upon all your mental capabilities to make decisions confidently, without second-guessing yourself, is evidence of reaching a personal level of success. I went on to say, the development of a positive attitude is step number one in any attempt to become successful.

I want you to feel successful, and I am telling you strength of mind is a huge component. So how do you build mental strength?

Strong mental capacity is a result of living, laughing and learning. In 1904, American poet, Bessie Anderson Stanley, wrote an oft-quoted and eloquent poem, "*Success*". The first line reads: *He has achieved success who has lived well, laughed often, and loved much.*

It reigns true.

As earlier mentioned, the *mental* aspect can be broken down into four components: clarity, learning, creativity, and entertainment. The fostering and development of each of these areas is where true mental strength lies.

Clarity

The intention is to live a life fulfilled and determine what that means. Clarity is having an understanding or perception, free from the chaos of confusion. Imagine the impact on your life if you were suddenly able to confidently make decisions without second guessing yourself. How much would things around you improve if you realized your power and the benefits of using it on a consistent basis?

Alex Morrison, the legendary golf instructor, said that *you must first see a thing in your mind before you can do it.* That, in itself, is clarity. Going from a point of clearly seeing and identifying what's real to you to putting it to work for yourself is a skill derived directly from mental strength.

Clarity is already in your grasp. Take responsibility to use your gift! The choice is yours to see what is in front of you. Oftentimes, we are the creators of our own confusion. Instead of seeing and believing, we see and question, unnecessarily. You are making the choice to be less clear when you associate yourself with people who lack clarity, allow yourself to be distracted by things that are not good for you, and surrender your power to substances promising you pleasure or power, but delivering you harm.

On the contrary, you increase your clarity by surrounding yourself with people with vision, people who are going places. When you are constantly learning, doing things that will move you forward, and putting things in your body to improve it, you are increasing your level of clarity.

Clarity is highly attainable; it's actually right before you, provided you're willing to do the work. Recall when I was in college and I had my breakdown. One major red flag evidencing itself was me piling more things on my plate than I could handle properly. I lacked confidence and clarity. I was clearly confused about what decisions needed to be made, and instead of using my power, I dulled it by creating chaos.

When you're working towards a goal, it's best to work one objective at a time. In doing so, you are keeping your path clear. You can see everything happening around you, and should things go awry in any way you will have the time and energy needed to correct it.

Clarity is a choice, one that I lacked the skills to make during college. I had taken mental health for granted and how clarity impacted my wellbeing. I had to learn these lessons on my own…and with some rather good counseling. Once I realized the importance, I knew I had to share the wealth.

Learning

The mind is like a muscle, use it or lose it! The same way you have to exercise your muscles, you need to do the same with your brain. After all, it is the control center of your body. The best way to do so is to *always be learning.*

After I started at the jewelry store, the years seemed to fly by, and my goal of returning to school became a thing of the past. Even so, I kept learning. I became a sponge to books and lectures. If a useful piece of knowledge was out there and I had access to its potential benefits, I wanted to learn. It was important for me to keep introducing myself to new improvements, procedures, and ideas.

My thirst for learning eventually landed me a position with a company that sought me out. Picture this, a high school graduate working alongside people with bachelor's and master's degrees, and I was doing extremely well. I ended up being a leader and business coach within the organization.

In addition to learning new ideas, you should also strengthen your current skills. Let's say you sew really well; you could set a goal to learn a new technique, or even create patterns. Push yourself to new heights. Constant challenge nurtures your mental strength.

Learning exercises your brain, and it also plays a pretty significant role in your overall life. By continuing to learn, you are preparing yourself to be adaptable. When you learn about new things, you open yourself up to new possibilities. For example, if you learn about Cuba and decide to explore the country, you are positively impacting the experience simply because you will know more about the cities, landscape and culture before you arrive.

Learning also helps you better respond to situations. Let's say you just watched a documentary about snake bites. Later, when one of your friends is bitten, you are able to make a well-informed and confident decision about how best to handle the bite. Obviously, this is an extreme example, but you get the idea. The more you learn, the more you know, and the more you can be of service—to yourself and others.

Creativity

Steve Jobs, founder of Apple and one of the most brilliant men to live, stated that *creativity is just connecting things. When you ask creative people how they did something, they feel a little guilty because they didn't really do it, they just saw something. It seemed obvious to them after a while. That's because they were able to connect experiences they've had and synthesize new things.* When I read this, I saw clarity, learning, and creativity. The clarity is in the ability to see a new way; the learning is being open to applying new thoughts; and the creativity is transforming what you see by putting it all together.

Imagine utilizing your power of clarity, learning every day, and giving yourself the freedom to be creative. How much more effective would you be? How much more fulfilled would you feel? I read once, being creative is getting over the fear of being wrong, and I agree. That is mental strength. All too often, we worry about how we will be perceived. All we should be concerned with is how we perceive ourselves, and doing all we need to ensure our self-perception is positive.

Some researchers believe creativity impacts mortality. Essentially, they're saying, being creative helps you live longer because of the impact it has on the brain. It also helps you solve problems, similar to learning but with an innovative spin. Creativity also builds confidence, empowering you to accomplish infinitely more.

So how do you become more creative? Ironically, you attain creativity through clarity and learning. You see how it all works together? And, while you're learning, you might choose to spend even more time studying related topics so you become an expert. The more you know about a single topic, the more equipped you are to be innovative in that area, and empowered to ask the questions needing to be asked to make it better. Ask questions, and then ask some more. It's in that hunger where you cultivate a creative spirit.

Creativity is a result of being open to new ideas and ways of thinking. It also comes from being aware and intentional. Spend some time with yourself, learn who you are and what you like, see the good, be a kid again. As simple as it sounds, personal historical reflection is effective.

When I had my poolside moment several years ago, I brain dumped. I allowed myself to empty my thoughts onto a page, then I organized them. The mental inventory I wrote is an example of creativity, because it allowed me to get here, to this conversation with you. One of the most powerful things you can do for yourself and others is to act on your creativity; someone will probably need what you've created.

Entertainment

On the flip side of creating art is pursuing the pleasure art can bring to your life. Brigham Young, a 19th century religious leader, stated that, *life is best enjoyed when time periods are evenly divided between labor, sleep and recreation...all people should spend one-third of their time in recreation which is rebuilding, voluntary activity, never idleness.*

Do we set aside time for recreation? We should, because it is during this time we rebuild. It is during this time we hit reset. Entertainment time lets our hair down and enjoy the fruits of our labor. Relaxation is necessary for our mental strength and overall mental health.

Now that you've experienced my presentation on the mental aspect, it's time for you to get reflective. Think back over what you've read, the components making up this aspect of your life, and determine how you stack up. Assess whether these facets are present in your life or if you should get to work implementing them.

As you consider the areas mentioned within the mental aspect, think of how you can fill your mental *happy account.* Remember, the more you intentionally fill your account with strengthening ideas and actions, the greater reserves you'll have to call upon when you have your greatest need.

Mental

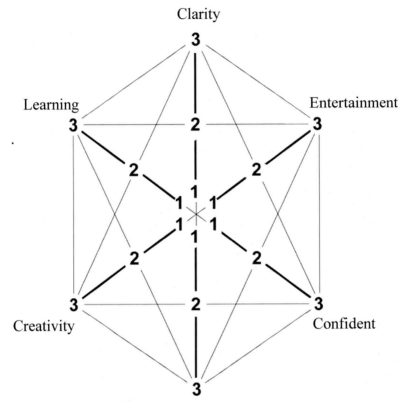

Clarity

Learning

Entertainment

Creativity

Confident

Use of mind-altering
substances under control

1 - Negative
2 - Neutral
3 - Positive

Physical

"Take care of your body. It's the only place you have to live."

-    Jim Rohn, Business Philosopher

Our body is a temple. Sounds cliché, right? Sure, because the statement is true! We get one-just one. And, over the course of our lives, we decide how to treat this irreplaceable vessel. We can treat our body as some magical self-healing instrument or we can provide ourselves top physical care. We have to put in the work for optimal physical performance, including regular physician visits and, minimizing mind-altering substances.

For optimization, we must eat well, be physically active, get ample sleep, and well, there is also an intimacy component. All of the above also play into our self-image.

Food & Beverage

With all the preservatives pumped into our foods, and chemicals sprayed over our foods, we have to watch our plates closely. What is advertised isn't always what is they say it is.

The more attention we pay to what goes into our body, the more control we have over what happens to our physical health.

Scientifically speaking, all human life originates from a single cell. And that cell has the ability to multiply; it also has the ability to repair itself. Some researchers say, cells are constantly working to create balance within the body. And guess what helps with that? Eating healthy.

The cells in our bodies literally have the ability to produce new cells, to heal damaged ones, or even replace them. And, we fuel it by what we put in our bodies.

According to Rath and Harter in *WellBeing,* we can silence our genes. Or at least there's the possibility. Many of us believe, if our father or grandfather had some malady, then we will be similarly afflicted. However, Rath and Harter's research shows that may not be true. We can actually impact what we're predisposed to by how we care for ourselves. And again, this comes largely as a result of what we eat and drink.

Exercise

I start most days with a bike ride or a swim. My friends and I are frequently planning trips to the mountains to hike. We understand the importance of physical activity. And I can tell you, I feel a difference now versus when I was less active.

It's amazing how doing more gives you energy to do more. And, doing less makes us feel sluggish. Funny how that works.

Exercise also plays a major role in our ability to self-heal. Regular physical activity strengthens our heart, as well as our entire cardiovascular system. It also helps with that pesky thing called stress.

Stress, although common, can worsen a variety of health issues from high blood pressure to heart disease, obesity and even diabetes. Contrary to popular belief, even a little bit of stress is not good.

Just a few minutes a day of activity to get the blood flowing is just what the doctor ordered. Most physicians suggest we get active at least thirty minutes each day for at least five days a week.

Go for a walk, or maybe a swim…or a bike ride! If you are the type that prefers a crowd to keep you motivated, try group exercise at your local gym.

It's actually quite comical how everything is so interconnected. People complain about issues they're having, not realizing that changing minor things could lead to a domino effect of results.

This is precisely why The SpiritPoint System is so important. We all need a system that will walk us through how to quickly check in with ourselves and identify the issue.

If I had a dollar for every time I heard someone say they didn't sleep well last night, I would have more money than I'd know what to do with. Sleep is so important, but slumber often seems to get interrupted, not started very well in the first place, or ended too early. Since sleep is one third of the components of good health (along with proper eating and exercise), the detriments of bad sleep cannot be overstated.

When your phone gets stuck or becomes unresponsive, what's the first action taken? Close down operations, hoping those brief moments, untouched, free of downloads, and free of activity will restore our communicator to a normal state. And, in most cases, voila! We have a well-functioning phone again!

We are our phones and sleep is our off button. A reset is necessary. Otherwise, we will get stuck, we will be non-responsive. We may even overheat and completely shut down like an overused phone!

For many of us, our phones are our life lines. They are how we stay connected with our families and the world. If they lose functionality, our day is thrown off drastically. We would have to quickly replace the phone so that those who need to contact us are able to.

If we broke down due to exhaustion, what would be different? How would the lives of those around us be impacted? If your life is anything remotely close to mine, being even slightly off your game causes alarm. Sleep is *one* of the ways to prevent this.

There are so many benefits to getting adequate rest, starting with improved memory. Many researchers even believe you may live longer. The major difference between us and our phones? They are replaceable. We are not.

Sleep also increases your creativity, and performance. Adequate sleep aids in weight loss, and reduces stress. See how everything is interconnected?

I can't discuss physical wellbeing without discussing intimacy. The reality? Sex *does* play a role in our physical wellbeing. It aids in the lowering of blood pressure, and it burns calories. So, on the most basic of levels, it constitutes as light exercise.

I feel obligated to add a disclaimer. *The intimacy I reference is one that takes place in healthy relationships.* It's important to add this disclaimer because in unhealthy situations, the benefits physically may not outweigh the detriment in other areas.

Sexual activity also affects your mental health, and although this section of the book is *physical-focused*, the mental benefits are important to include here as well.

Studies indicate sex can lead to increased levels of trust between you and your partner and to overall love in your relationship. Researchers also suggest sex can improve your ability to explore your emotions -to feel them, to identify the distinction between love and lust, and to communicate them effectively.

Sex is also thought to boost confidence. Imagine the impact on your life if you're eating right, you're physically active, you're sleeping well, and you're able to maintain an active sex life. Chances are your physical wellbeing will be at an all-time high.

It's that time again. Time for you to get real with yourself and your intentions for your physical wellbeing. Take a look at your self- assessment on the following page and ask; am I taking care of myself? Can you say yes emphatically, or do you need to think about it? How seriously are you taking the vessel that you, literally, only get one of? What are you doing daily to add to the *happy account* of your physical wellbeing?

Physical

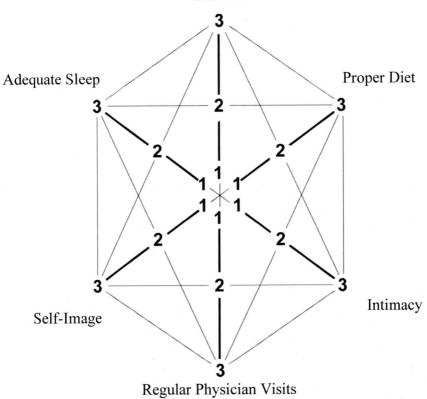

Exercise

Adequate Sleep

Proper Diet

Self-Image

Intimacy

Regular Physician Visits

1 - Negative
2 - Neutral
3 - Positive

World

"Though we travel the world over to find the beautiful, we must carry it with us or we find it not."

- Ralph Waldo Emerson, Essayist, Poet

Our worlds are broken down into the people we know and those we don't. According to Rath and Harter in *Wellbeing,* our most memorable experiences, whether positive or negative, include at least one other person. And, if true, we can assume we *need* people, in one way or another.

Think back to the poolside experience. I swam alone, but my joy was the result of everything else happening in my life with my career, family, and the other SpiritPoint aspects.

Even when I was on the green, the detail of that story making it so powerful, was my sleeping friends lying around me. Those sleeping guys were so polar opposite of the direction my life needed to move in, yet so instrumental to me getting through some extremely difficult moments. They were monumental to my story even if they didn't continue to play a role.

People are all around us; they are influencing us, our decisions, and sometimes, our goals. They are shaping our views and impacting our moods. And, guess what? We have the same influence on them.

The Inner Circle

The inner circle is made up of two parts. First, your *brain-trust*. Your friends, colleagues, organizational associates, clergy, advisors, even your gym buddies make up the group you can usually count on for life's important moments and decisions. You've developed relationships with your *brain-trust*. You guys have built a rapport and have attained certain levels of trust.

Second, your *acquaintances*. The group of people you know, but have yet to develop a relationship with them. The guy in shipping and receiving, the letter carrier, the sweet lady at the cafeteria who serves you breakfast each morning. You know them, but they aren't in your *brain-trust*.

Your *brain-trust* understands you to some degree. Many members of your personal nexus can anticipate certain things about your behavior, and chances are, you see them regularly, or at least more often than not.

The Outer Circle

This is the dynamic group of individuals you don't know. Either you've yet to meet them or you have only seen them in passing. Perhaps you'll never meet them. They are the group you passed in the mall on Saturday, some poor soul in a breadline, the guy who sat next to you in the coffee shop.

The outer circle isn't familiar with you. They don't understand you or the nuances of your life. Quite frankly, they just don't know you, and you don't know them. Beth, working the drive thru at Starbucks, is completely unaware you are running late for a meeting. John, some guy in a sports car in front of you who can't get in touch with his wife, is driving erratically.

We spend our lives interacting with people. We are in charge of making those interactions positive, neutral, or negative.

You're running late for a meeting, and you committed yourself to bringing the group coffee. The line is long as usual this time of morning. And, at the passing of each moment, you're becoming more and more agitated.

By the time you reach the window, the frustration in your mind has manifested into a scowl on your face. Beth says good morning, but all you hear is the ticking of the second hand on the clock in your mind. In your rush, you snatch the tray of coffees and nearly spill them all.

Ironically enough, Beth's first week was in full manic swing and the car line made her a bit nervous. Her encounter with you really sent her over; she ended up having to retreat to the restroom to avoid a breakdown in front of her coworkers.

You arrive to your meeting, and everyone's excited to get started. They are standing around chatting, unbothered by the five minutes you're behind. Meanwhile, Beth is still in the restroom in tears.

Neutral Interactions

In the neutral space, you aren't propelling things forward, but at least you aren't sending young girls to the bathroom in tears. Consider John, who is in a hurry to get home to his expectant wife. Instead of hurling an expletive at his swerving car, you don't respond. You don't allow it to affect your mood, one way or another. It just is what it is, right?

The neutral space is the middle of the road and on the cusp of improvement. You have total control over the type of adjustments you can make.

Pleasant Interactions

When you have the choice to be *anything*, why would you choose anything other than positive? That's a serious question. Why would anybody choose to decrease when they have the power and the ability to increase pleasantness around themselves?

Being pleasant is exactly what it sounds like. It's finding the good. It's smiling despite what you may be feeling inside. It's speaking even when you don't know the face in front of you. Pleasant interactions occur when the you build people up during those moments you might otherwise not bother. A bit of extra pleasantry brings you a sense of feeling good and fueled to multiply the goodness in the lives of those around you.

The Network

The dictionary defines a network as a group of interconnected people or things. During my financial services career, I learned, networking was essential to growing my practice. The people I helped to grow their business helped me do the same. Our connections were crucial in expanding our spheres of influence.

Personally speaking, wealth isn't just the money you have in the bank. It is the value in everything around you. So, if your network influences such thinking, imagine the value you can add to other people's lives and them to yours.

Sure, you'll meet some people who may find themselves on the neutral spectrum, unable to push you forward or backwards. However, what about you and your effect on their lives?

All interactions matter and we all should make conscious efforts to be more intentional in our connections with others. Rather than acting out of a sense of self, we should remain open to the possibilities of helping someone in a meaningful way. Even the simple pleasure of putting a smile on someone's face is a moment of inspiration. Imagine the domino effect of actions on their day, giving them the chance to forward that positive feeling. And the fellow in the breadline? Perhaps he is your call to expand the network of good you can bring to the world. Are you charitably inclined?

Our networks make us rich. They fuel and feed the areas of our lives, and they are directly related to the relationships we *have* and continue to *build.*

What's your place in the world? Are you putting out positive vibes, as the kids are saying these days, or are you emitting toxic energy? Are you interconnecting with people to help foster the greater good? Do you pick up a piece of trash and put it in the wastebasket? Do you reach out to new people to expand your inner circle?

Right now is the most opportune time to be honest with yourself. Which of the six areas noted in the World diagram give you opportunity to fill your *happy account?*

World

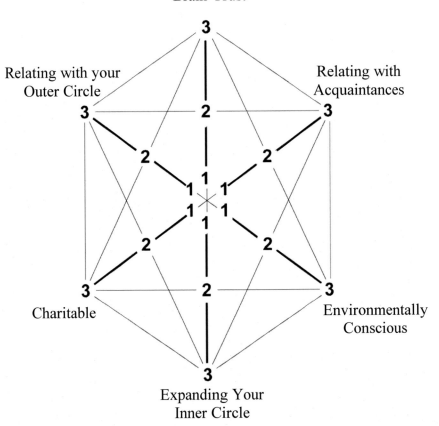

Relating with Your
Brain-Trust

Relating with your
Outer Circle

Relating with
Acquaintances

Charitable

Environmentally
Conscious

Expanding Your
Inner Circle

1 - Negative
2 - Neutral
3 - Positive

Family

"Family is not an important thing. It's everything."

- Michael J. Fox, Actor

"Family Ties" isn't just a television show from the 1980's. How well do you connect with your spouse, children, parents and siblings? What is your interaction with in-laws, uncles, aunts, cousins and others you consider as family? How does your family tie together? No matter how you categorize them, they all play an integral role in your overall well-being, at least to a certain degree.

Life is about experiences, good and bad. They can be intensified by the presence of our loved ones. When you find yourself in the midst of a not-so-good experience, your family can be there to provide love, support, and coaching. They can be there to help you win or pick you up after a fall.

Throughout my childhood, the importance of family was always clear. Depending on which circumstance I found myself encountering, the closeness or distance to a particular family member would ebb or increase. The one constant was always love, no matter the situation.

I relished the intricacies of my family members as they all provided a view into myself I wouldn't have otherwise seen. My dad walked out onto the porch each morning to pray and it always made me feel good to see him commune with God. My Mom was extremely purposeful about her art and social justice. One sister was the picture of positivity, no matter the circumstance. My other sister's artistic abilities left me in awe of her genius.

All of their nuances helped mold me into the friend, husband, and father I am today. I wouldn't be who I am without them being who they are. Looking back on my childhood makes me grateful.

One tradition from childhood my sisters and I observed was our connection together on Friday nights. Despite the disruptions I experienced at age fifteen, one activity seemed to always find itself as a constant; lighting Sabbath candles together on Friday nights. With the onset of smart phones, we've started to share photos from our Friday night gatherings, even over time zones. Sharing our Friday evenings together electronically is our way of saying *wish you were here*!

Family can be quite the challenge. You don't always like each other. So, if you've been thinking about some negative family issues while you've been reading, no worries. You're not alone! But, not liking them doesn't make them any less family.

I feel we have obligations to ourselves, to our family members, and the world to continue to bond, even with those we dislike. Because, in that bonding, in that connection, you just might find the root of your dislike. And, maybe you can influence a positive outcome, an action that may never happen if you don't take the time.

There's a saying that *a family that prays together stays together*. I agree, but allow me to make it wider. A family that interacts and experiences together strengthens their connections. They make themselves more impactful in each other's lives. Ultimately, they deposit positivity in each other's *happy account*, providing a place from which to draw when the time calls for it.

Remember when I said there's a 100% chance that bad outcomes will happen at some point in your life? Well, guess who will be there for you? Your family. And, defining your family is your call! Yes, there are the biological, obvious people we all know as family. Perhaps you have brought someone from your inner circle you have declared family as well. Just like everything else, there's give and take. Where do you stack up with family in filling your *happy account?*

Family

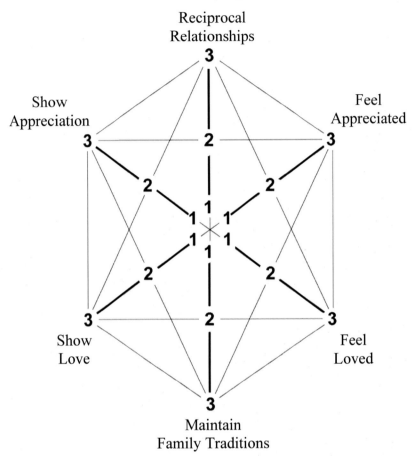

Reciprocal Relationships

Show Appreciation

Feel Appreciated

Show Love

Feel Loved

Maintain Family Traditions

1 - Negative
2 - Neutral
3 - Positive

Career

"A career is like a house: it's made of many bricks, and each brick has the same value, because without any one of them, the house would collapse."

- Andrea Bocelli, Blind Songwriter

I have a niece, let's call her Sally Boswell, who is, what I call a rare duck. At seven years old, she proudly and confidently stated her claim on her life. She wanted to be a pediatric nurse, and 27 years later, she is just that. She's a rarity, because oftentimes the dreams we have as children change several times over.

We start out wanting to be a superhero. Over time, that becomes fire fighter, and somewhere along the way we settle into comfy positions as accountants, financial analysts, teachers, or the like. That's just life for most of us.

Not Sally. She knew. I admire her for knowing, and I admire her even more for sticking to her nursing career aspirations. For the rest of us who have ideas but aren't quite sure, we just keep moving forward. Career can be broken down into two separate yet interdependent parts: pre-graduation and post-graduation.

When you are a student, your career is to learn. I define career as that which will help you financially sustain yourself. Sure, you may still need the support of parents and/or guardians, but the reality is you won't always have them to pay your way. With time, you draw the line in the sand separating you as a child from you as an adult.

When you concentrate on your education, you are setting the foundation of your career. Studying takes intentionality, preparing you to be successful. Proper schooling makes you better suited to choose a career that lights your fire versus a drudgery you *have* to do.

I am sure you noticed, so far there is no mention of *job*. It's with good reason, the main one being, I despise that word. There's no future in it. It's simply a copout you've committed to doing for a check, whereas, a career is always preparing you for the next phase in your life. The actions in your vocation may be the same either way. However, if you

140

perform those actions as a 'job', you aren't looking forward. 'Career' means you perform the duties at hand, but look to improve them or rise up to a better position. The difference between job and career is your mindset. Jobs suck. Careers rock.

Look again at the SpiritPoint diagram. You will see career at the foundation. The quality of your life rests on your ability to happily bring home an income. When you are preparing yourself for financial independence, you are drawing upon the other five aspects of life. And when you're stable financially, you're able to add exponential value to the other areas.

Your career can be like a fountain or a drain. Pursuing financial success can provide many wonders flowing into your life. Conversely, your mental, emotional and time resources can get sucked into a never-ending hole.

In addition to being intentional in our education pursuits, we must also be open to potentially new ideas. When I started at the junior college, I had all the intentions of becoming a lawyer. As life turned out, the universe had a different path in mind for me.

After I got sick and returned home, reluctantly, I began to work in the family jewelry store. During those twelve years, I became obsessed with jewelry design, earning a reputation as a respected gemologist. In the process of this unexpected turn of events, I met people who saw qualities in me leading them to believe I might be successful in finance. Soon after, I found myself spending the next thirty years as a financial advisor and asset manager. See, when you keep moving forward, and remain open, magic can happen.

Post-Graduation

Some years ago, I was advising a client, a young man in his mid-thirties. I'll call him Jerry Purcell. He was a successful and entrepreneurial salesman with a leading printing company. We were working on his portfolio and I saw special potential in him.

Jerry cared about people. He was extremely organized and he had the gift of gab. He always asked good questions showcasing his attention to detail.

So, I asked him if he would be open to a career in the financial services industry. Initially, he looked at me in shock. He didn't have an educational background in finance. He thought I was nuts for even asking him a question he perceived as silly. But, I saw a special fire in him.

Jerry is now a top financial advisor for one of my company's best competitors. And, he's maintained that position for several years running.

I bet you're wondering why I turned him over to a competitor, aren't you? The answer? He had characteristics better suited for their clientele. I saw specific abilities in Jerry, and instead of performing an action benefitting me and my interests, I served his. And as a result, he's flourished. You might say, I 'phase-four-religioned' him! I met him where he was. And here we've learned, when we continue moving forward, people notice us, just as I noticed Jerry.

Life has shown us, not everyone's story will be this easy. However, your life doesn't have to be much different. Whatever your position, treat your work like a career. Look at it as if you're a business of one, contracting your services out in return for a paycheck and benefits.

We've all seen the movies where a guy in the mailroom works his way up to CEO. Stories like that aren't just in the movies. Great opportunities are possible in our lives as well. No matter your role, pay attention to your surroundings, and work hard to learn new ways to create a benefit of some kind every day. Ask questions, and answer them too. Show you've been paying attention. Trust me - your hard work will get noticed.

No matter how humble your position, perform with honor. And always remember to look next to you. Not up. Not down. Always next. No one is above or below you. We are walking together, and the sooner you realize this, the easier your conversation with anybody will be, no matter their background or position.

In 1972, eight students across the United States were recognized at the White House for work they had done in their communities. I was among that eight. As a member of the high school council, I worked tirelessly to ensure our paper drive was successful. Our results were far beyond what any of us could have imagined.

During this time, Richard Nixon was president. Unfortunately, there was a national emergency needing immediate attention during our ceremony. So, instead of having the award presented to me by the President, his daughter, Julie, was the presenter. Still, an honor, obviously. Just not the same.

For about ten years, that award sat in a drawer. One day, I decided I was going to get Mr. Nixon's signature. I called the White House at a time when Ronald Reagan was in charge. I spoke to the switch board operator and asked how I could reach the former President. She gave me the phone number of Mr. Nixon's executive assistant. I made the call.

I explained to his right-hand confidant what happened. While I was there with fellow students from across the land, Mr. Nixon had gotten tied up with an emergency event related to the War in Vietnam. Hence, no signature from the President of the United States. I could hear the apprehension in her voice about this unlikely story, especially calling ten years later. But, I was determined.

I asked her to please just relay the message. I held the phone while she left to speak with the former President. She returned to the phone a few minutes later to say he remembered the day and asked me to drop the certificate in the mail. Within weeks, I had my signed certificate in hand.

I told this story to a young man from Ghana. He was my mentee and I was advising him on ways to navigate life in America. Obtaining a letter of introduction from his country's most famous world figure would have been a huge boost for his employment options. He told me getting such a letter would be ridiculously hard. After all, my mentee was just an exchange student and the political figure was larger than life. With that excuse, I walked him back to my office and showed him the Nixon certificate. I reminded him, he walks NEXT to the world figure. Not up, Not below. Even if the political figure failed to return his correspondence, at least he would get over his belief he was somehow not worthy to contact the great man.

Securing a career is just the tip of the iceberg. Finding a career you love is great. Still, you must live off its fruits and allow it to secure your future.

Too many people make money matters very complicated. Handling your personal finances can be very emotional and a source of grief or a simple exercise in mathematics. When understood simply in logical terms, handling your expenses and savings just becomes another exercise in making your life better.

I've been teaching financial literacy since 1987, and bringing money knowledge to people still excites me. The key to having enough money for the rest of your life is proper planning. You must manage your spending, invest wisely, and save for a rainy day (and the sunshine for that matter) while minimizing your liabilities. As such, I have created categories I like to call *spending buckets.*

Bucket #1: Monthly Spending

Post-graduation is when life gets real for most of us. That's when we accumulate expenses. And as we get older, either the number of expenses goes up or the dollar amount does, or both. These expenses are in the monthly spending bucket. Every thirty days, expect an invoice.

Bucket #2: Yearly Spending

In addition to the money we spend on a recurring monthly basis, we also have expenses expected to occur throughout the year. The family vacation, swimming pool lessons, and car maintenance are examples of activities or purchases you know will come up over the next twelve months. Previewing the upcoming year will prepare you for annual expenses.

Bucket #3: One Year and Beyond

Let's take planning a step further and provide for needs and wishes we would like to see happen within three years. Perhaps you want to buy a house, and want to save for a down-payment. Or maybe you are super detailed and are anticipating a large expense. Perhaps your old car is ready to be retired or your air-conditioning unit is due for replacement.

You could literally open an account for each category and set up drafts, if you so choose, from your main checking account. The reality is the expense will come whether you're prepared or not. So why not be prepared?

The purpose of the "bucket" system is to be prepared. You're constantly and consistently pouring funds into these buckets, small amounts at a time, that will later allow you to act in peace. Like the others, you can set up a fund covering things like a blown tire or your kid's baseball through the neighbor's window. You could even take a look back over the last few years at "stuff" that has happened, and predict a dollar amount that works for your life. Obviously, a parent of four growing children would have a different dollar amount than a young person who is fresh out of college.

You might not know *what* "stuff" will happen, but you can bet, "stuff" *will* happen. Instead of dealing with unexpected "stuff" on a whim, plan for these eventual expenses.

And speaking of planning, money matters connect to the other five aspects in an unbelievable way. When you have planned and are prepared for the expense, stress is at a minimum which in turn allows you to continue pouring positive energy into your spirituality, family matters, physical well-being, mental health, and the world around you.

When your finances are in good order, your career can soar since money-worry distractions are minimized. If you have ever wondered how the rich get richer and the poor get poorer, here's a hint. The rich tend to be better organized which allows them the opportunity to get richer.

Investments

Your career should allow you to take care of yourself now and *later.* Truth is, one day we all want to be able to kick our feet up and live off the fruits of our labor; maybe even begin a less lucrative career, because we can. Thus, we must invest. I liken this process to building an avatar.

Remember in the movie, "Avatar," the people created a new being that could do things for them they couldn't do for themselves? That's what your investments should do for you. When you can no longer (or choose to no longer) earn money, it's important to have built an investment program that produces income to sustain you, post-retirement.

Investment accounts such as IRA, 401(k), or personal savings can and should be there for you later in life. Remember this about life: the first third is growing up. The second third is doing what you have to do. And, the last third is doing what you want to do. To do what you want to do requires you to build your financial avatar.

Debt

Debt is the greatest inhibitor to personal financial growth. Owing money is one topic that really grinds my gears. I know in many cases, you can't avoid borrowing money. But, oftentimes you can put off a purchase which assigns you the position of debtor.

Over the last few pages, I've been telling you about this bucket system and I strongly believe in the effectiveness of this discipline. Here's why: we are always going to need food, clothing, housing...the list goes on. That won't likely change for the foreseeable future. The problem comes when we foresee the need for wants and needs and decide not to plan for those expenses.

Instead, we use credit card and loans, most of which have astronomical interest rates. In many instances, we *could* have just poured some money into one of those buckets back there and avoided paying more to get less. Consider this example for further study:

Your repair guy tells you your air conditioner unit will have to be replaced in three years. He also tells you the expense will be around $10,000. You now have two choices: You can either start pouring money into your *One Year and Beyond* bucket or you can wait three years and charge that expense on a credit card.

If you choose the first option, you can begin to set aside $300 per month over the next thirty-four months. And, when the unit goes out, you simply repair it with peace of mind. Or, you can do nothing over the next thirty-four months and use that credit card when the time comes for the repairs.

In the second option, you'll have a $300 payment for forty-one months (instead of thirty-four) since you'll also own an extra $2,417 in interest charges due to the 12.9% annual percentage interest rate the credit card will charge. Hmmm, what's in YOUR wallet...?

Hopefully, you can see which is the better option. If the difference is unclear, let me further clarify. Three years ago, you knew the AC repair was coming, right? If you choose option two, you now have three more years to worry about that same thing. You've now doubled the time you've had to think about that unit, and to boot, you've put yourself in debt $2,417 *extra* dollars. See why I dislike debt?

All that said, mortgages are a bit different. Think of them as poodles with a muzzle versus other debt being Rottweilers unleashed. Let me explain. With a mortgage, you're protected from increasing interest rates, you have a set number of payments, and your interest rates are typically lower.

The cherry on top? Mortgage interest may be tax deductible. And, here's another secret of smart personal money managers: They pay down their mortgages faster than required. Why? Because just like the poodle and Rottweiler are both dogs, debt is debt. And, when you can be totally debt-free, there's a *freedom* that can't be explained. Still, I must admit, I really do love dogs, just not debt.

The stability of your finances dictates the stability of the Six Aspect of Life. That's why *Career* is on the bottom of the diagram. It is your financial foundation. Is your base sturdy? Are you soaring or is this area the root of issues plaguing your family, spirituality, mental health, physical well-being, and/or the world around you?

The *happy accounts* mentioned throughout SpiritPoint are based on real-life savings and investment accounts.

Imagine, as you fill your financial accounts, that they can provide you a buffer just like all the other *happy accounts*. How are you filling your career *happy accounts*?

Career

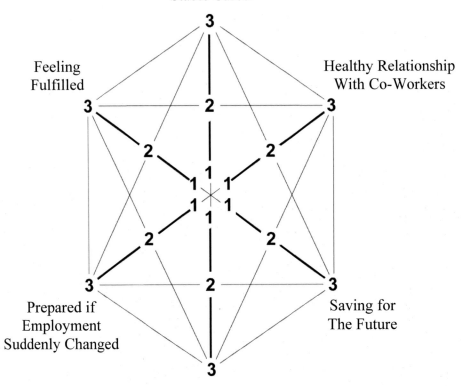

Stable Career

Feeling Fulfilled

Healthy Relationship With Co-Workers

Prepared if Employment Suddenly Changed

Saving for The Future

Financially Secure

1 - Negative
2 - Neutral
3 - Positive

Conclusion and Post Assessment

"A single day is enough time to make us a little larger or, another time, a little smaller."

    -    Paul Klee, early 20th Century Artist

All Six Aspects of Life are interconnected. The SpiritPoint symbol's design purposely joins all six aspects to each other to demonstrate how they feed into one another. I like to say, *One feeds five. Five feeds one.* Recognizing the interconnection of all life's aspects, and the areas within, is the first step in allowing you to better fulfill your purpose in life. The remaining steps involve you working the program each day in some meaningful way. Remember, you direct life or circumstances direct you.

As Paul Klee stated, *a single day is enough time to make us a little larger or, another time, a little smaller.* Whatever we need to be, we have the power to be. We just have to take the time to look at ourselves, our lives, and the content within our own six aspects. Then, we have to do the work needed to get us to more purposeful living.

Existing in purpose means you are present. You are positively impacting specific areas of your life while simultaneously impacting the others as well. Existing by chance means you are floating. You are allowing the waves of life to move you to and fro, with minimal intervention on your part. Which way do YOU choose?

You began this journey with an open mind, or at least that's my hope. Now, here you are at the end of the book, yet not even close to the end of your journey. When I think about the SpiritPoint System, I hope more people will become deliberative and reflective with the intention of taking their existence further.

Self-improvement and personal development do not happen overnight. The experience is entirely yours. I am just here to facilitate the process as best I can. I know all too well what it feels like to be low, and I also know the joy of being fulfilled. And, that fulfillment has led me to you.

Until now, I've only facilitated this program in person. As I'm sure you can guess, relying on in-person presentations has limited who could hear and read this message. The candid conversations I've had with audience members, in addition to the looks on their faces when a certain aspect of life would click personally for them, lit a fire under me to get these ideas into your hands. Euphoria or happiness with how you live isn't some far-fetched dream. Good outcomes are achievable for us all. We just have to be intentional in our efforts to get there. That said, I hope you and I will meet one day at a conference or webinar. It would be my greatest pleasure to interact with you personally should you so desire. Remember my call to Mr. Nixon?

At the beginning of the book, you assessed yourself across the Six Aspects of Life. You then went through each aspect and the areas within them. The time has come for you to repeat the overview process of the Six Aspects. Now is the opportunity to see how your attitude about life's many parts might have adjusted. Has the shape of the wheel improved? Is it a little less bumpy?

Six Aspects of Life – Post-Assessment

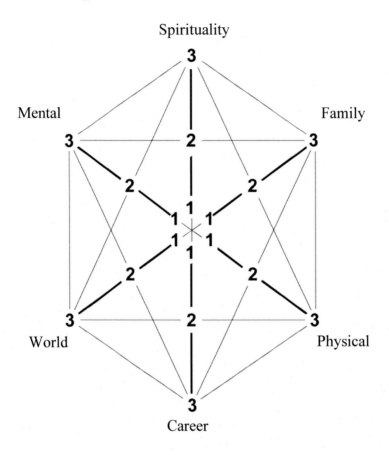

1 - Negative
2 - Neutral
3 - Positive

A Call to Action

By creating the SpiritPoint System, I drew a line in the sand between an existence by chance and one by purpose. In one working document, you have at your fingertips, the tools needed to organize your thoughts, perceive your strengths and challenges, and a process to reveal your own hidden opportunities. The goal? To facilitate putting into action what you perceive as your purpose in life. Since you now have this instrument in hand, get to know the powers within your six aspects, put them into action, and go make life happen YOUR way!!

Acknowledgements

Since the early 1990's, several audiences (one-on-one and group settings) have been instrumental in allowing me to hone this project into a viable and useful endeavor. I'm constantly humbled by the way others take the precepts of SpiritPoint and find ways to teach me new forms of applying its principles.

In the spirit of *World* and *Family*, I hereby fully acknowledge, many people who have participated in the development of this effort are left out of this acknowledgement, only because I'm drawing from an errant and selective memory. If you have contributed to the creation of SpiritPoint, please know in your own heart how important your contribution has been, even though I've failed to cite your efforts.

In the summer of 2017 when I decided it was finally time to organize the SpiritPoint System into the written word, I was blessed to find an organized, smart, energetic, and insightful collaborator in the form of Laneshia Lamb. She and I spent countless hours laying out the most effective ways to communicate a process which I had heretofore done only in-person. Laneshia's writing skills have provided the cohesion needed to effectively communicate to a wider audience my heretofore very personalized way of expressing SpiritPoint principles and the magic it brings to people's lives. I'm eternally grateful for her ear, mind, and soul as the combo responsible for producing what you read today.

Several wonderful guides have taken time, effort, and care to read the SpiritPoint System before having it published. Each in their own way has contributed to presenting its message in the most effective way possible. Alphabetically, they are Chelsea Alexander, Dr. Abigail Brenner, Rev. Sharon Cantrell, Bishop Brian Farrell, Dr. Tahita Fulkerson, Rev. Charles F. Johnson, Ilana Knust, Tatiana Miller, Art Mortell, Brent and Jeri Peterson, Paul R.

Ray, Jr., Vernon E. Rew, Jr., Rabbi David Rosen, Dr. Michael Ross, Chad Sanschagrin, Scott Sherwin, Dr. Newell Williams, Rev. Chris Wilson, Pouya Yadegar, Rabbi Brian Zimmerman, and Saul Zimmerman.

It would be remiss to go without acknowledging Billy Greenberg and Debby Rice, who were instrumental in the development of the SpiritPoint symbol.

Of course, my ever-patient and cheerleading wife, Julie Goldstein and our three sons, Andy Goldstein, David Goldstein, and Jacob Fuld have all stood by my side offering encouragement over the years. I also want to acknowledge my first wife, Suzanne, as she continuously encouraged me to develop the SpiritPoint System in its early years of formation.

Daniel J. Red Goldstein

Red is a fourth-generation native of Fort Worth, Texas. His early career was with his family's business, Goldstein Brothers Jewelers, where he became a gemologist, jewelry designer and appraiser. In 1987, at age 32, he was recruited by Merrill Lynch where he became a financial advisor and portfolio manager for private clients and the firm's trust company. In 2009, he and his partners started their own firm, TeakTree Capital Management, LLC. In 2013, he became an ambassador for the firm while simultaneously starting SpiritPoint Coaching & Consulting, LLC. Red is married to the former Julie Krauss of Fort Worth. Together, their blended family consists of three sons, Andy Goldstein, David Goldstein and Jacob Fuld.